PICTURE JOKES for KIDS

by
ROY MITCHELL

WARD LOCK LIMITED · LONDON

TO VERONICA, DAN, LU-LU AND ROSIE
FOR PUTTING UP WITH IT.

© ROY MITCHELL 1986

FIRST PUBLISHED IN GREAT BRITAIN IN 1986
BY WARD LOCK LIMITED, 8 CLIFFORD STREET,
LONDON WIX IRB, AN EGMONT COMPANY.

REPRINTED 1987

PRINTED IN GREAT BRITAIN
BY WILLIAM CLOWES LTD,
BECCLES

BRITISH LIBRARY CATALOGUING IN PUBLICATION DATA

PICTURE JOKES FOR KIDS
 1. WIT AND HUMOUR, JUVENILE 2. ENGLISH
 WIT AND HUMOUR
 I. MITCHELL, ROY
 828'.91402'0809282   PZ8.7

ISBN 0-7063-6472-4

WARNING!

THE JOKES IN THIS BOOK COULD SERIOUSLY DAMAGE YOUR BRAIN!!

Stupid Sid

PERCY PIGG

LOOPY LULU...

FAT MATT

GHOSTLY GAGS

...and Lots More!

Stupid

Sid....

Stupid Sid's CROSSWORD PUZZLE

DOWN

1 SID'S NAME
2 SID'S NAME
3 SID'S NAME
4 SID'S NAME
5 SID'S NAME
6 SID'S NAME

ACROSS

1 SID'S NAME
3 SID'S NAME
4 SID'S NAME
5 SID'S NAME
7 SID'S NAME
8 SID'S NAME
9 SID'S NAME

NO CHEATING!! (SOLUTION ON PAGE

Stupid Sid - the DOZY KID!

LOONY LIMERICK!

There was an old lady from Dover
Who decided to knit a pullover—
But would you believe
She knitted four sleeves,
And now it only fits Rover!

Granny at 6 months

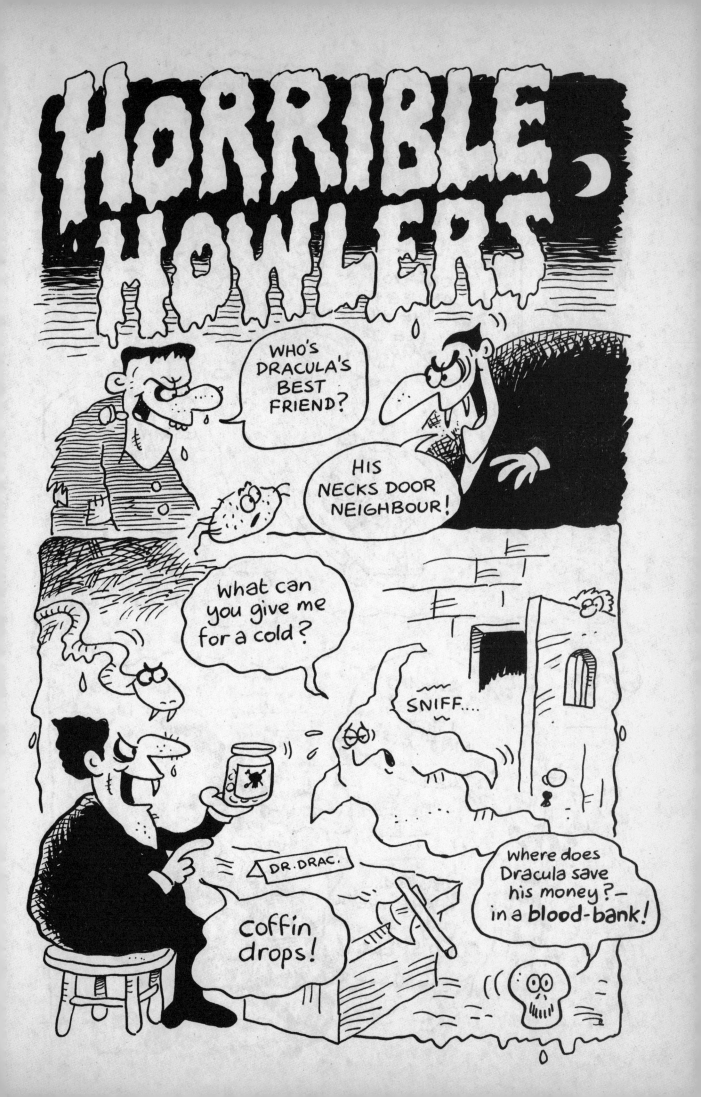

STUPID SID......

WHAT HAS TWO ARMS, TWO WINGS, EIGHT LEGS, TWO TAILS, THREE HEADS, AND THREE BODIES?

A MAN ON AN ELEPHANT, HOLDING A PARROT!

did you hear about...

... the featherweight boxer who tickled his opponents to death?

... the man who went to a Fancy Dress Party dressed as a biscuit? — a dog ate him up in the hall!

yum!

... the man who kept his wife under the bed, because he thought she was a little potty?

... the man who set fire to his jacket because he wanted a blazer?

... the stupid optician? — he made a spectacle of himself!

I AMA PROPE RTW IT !

CRAZY CAROL

(SUNG TO THE TUNE OF 'WE THREE KINGS')

SERVICE WITH A SMILE!

ANIMAL-ANTICS!!

SIGN LANGUAGE

SILLY STRIPS

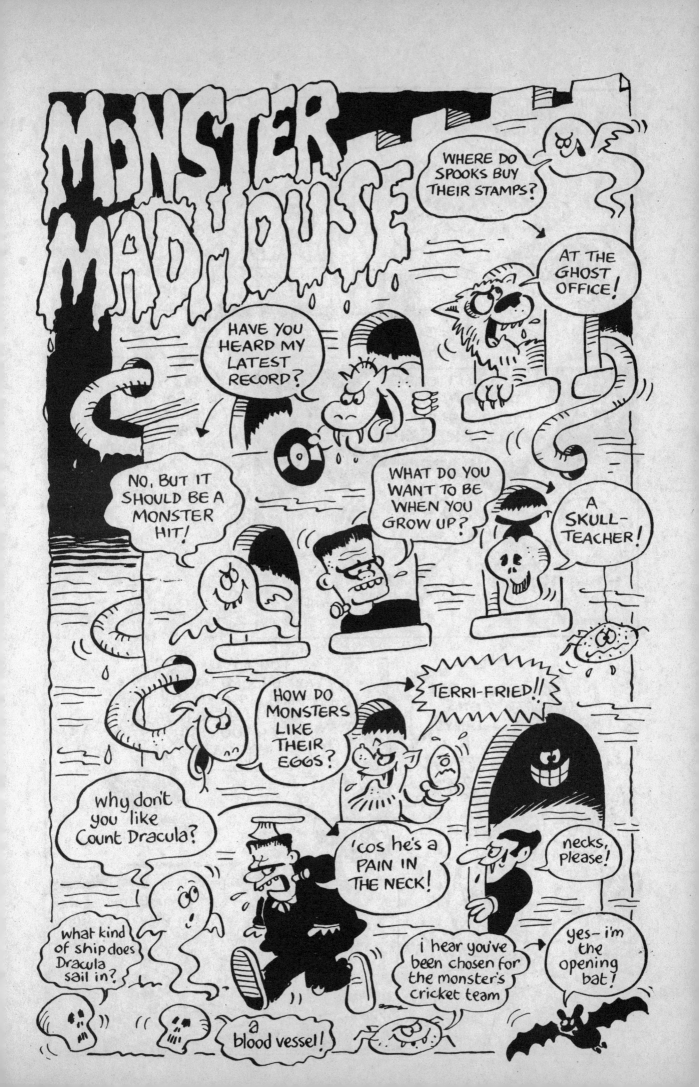

Did you hear about...

... the idiot who worked in a banana warehouse? — he was sacked for throwing the bent ones away!

no — they're no good..

... the man who slept with his head **under** the pillow? — when he woke up, the fairies had taken all his teeth out!!

... the boy scout who lost his beret in a cow field, and tried on 27 before he found it??!

Very a-moo-sing!

Stupid Sid's ? PUZZLE PAGE ?

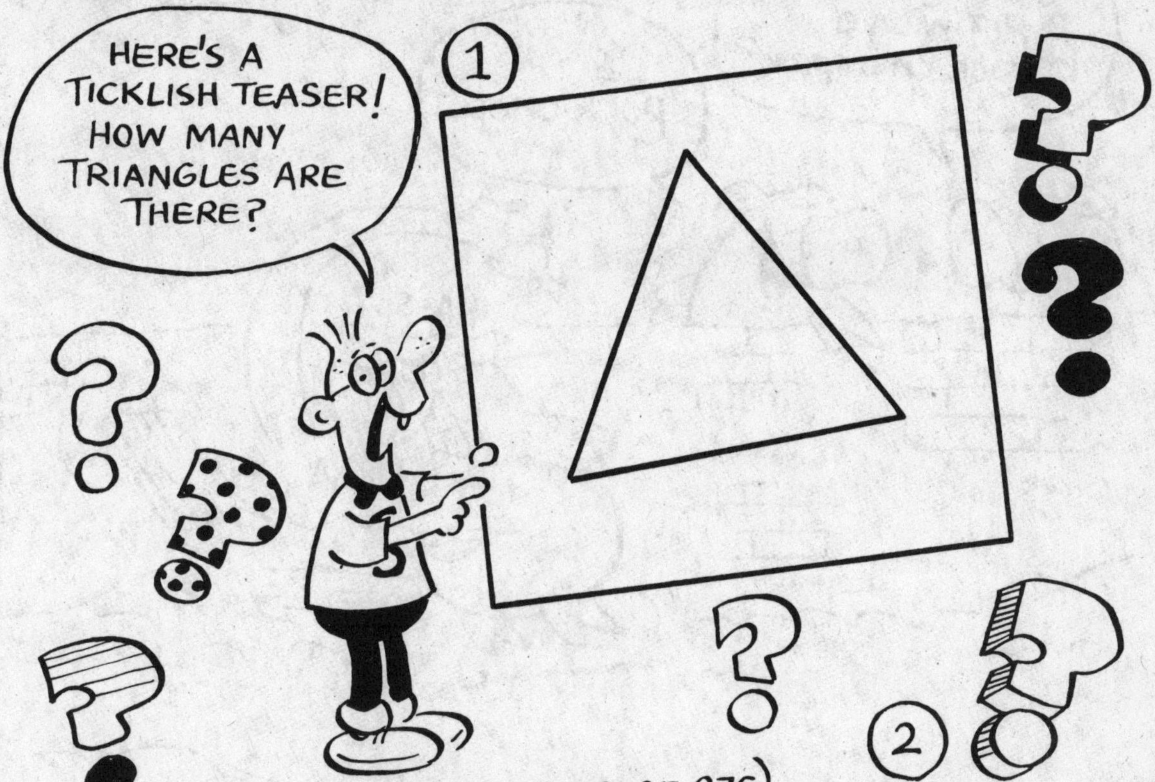

(ANSWERS ON PAGE 275)

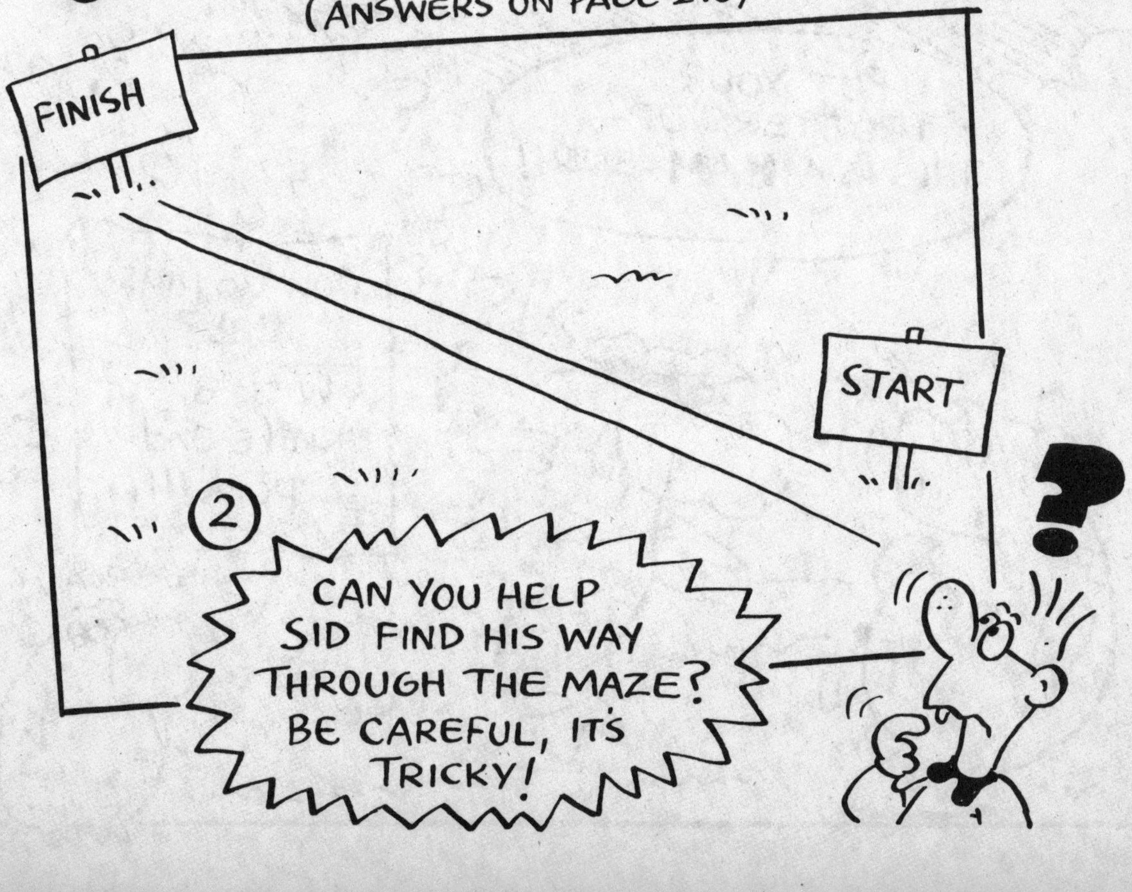

PERCY PIGG'S PORKY PAGE

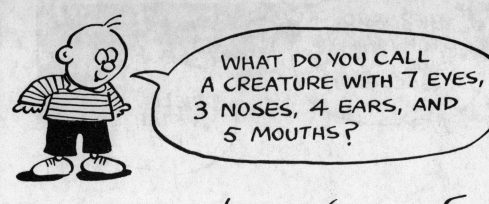

School Fun!!

HICKORY DICKORY DOCK,
THE ELEPHANT RAN UP THE CLOCK–

THE CLOCK IS NOW BEING REPAIRED!

DOUBLE-TAKE!!

Silly Strips......

Stupid Sid's PUZZLE PAGE! [no. 2]

I say, WAITER!

NEWS FLASH
from AUSTRALIA....

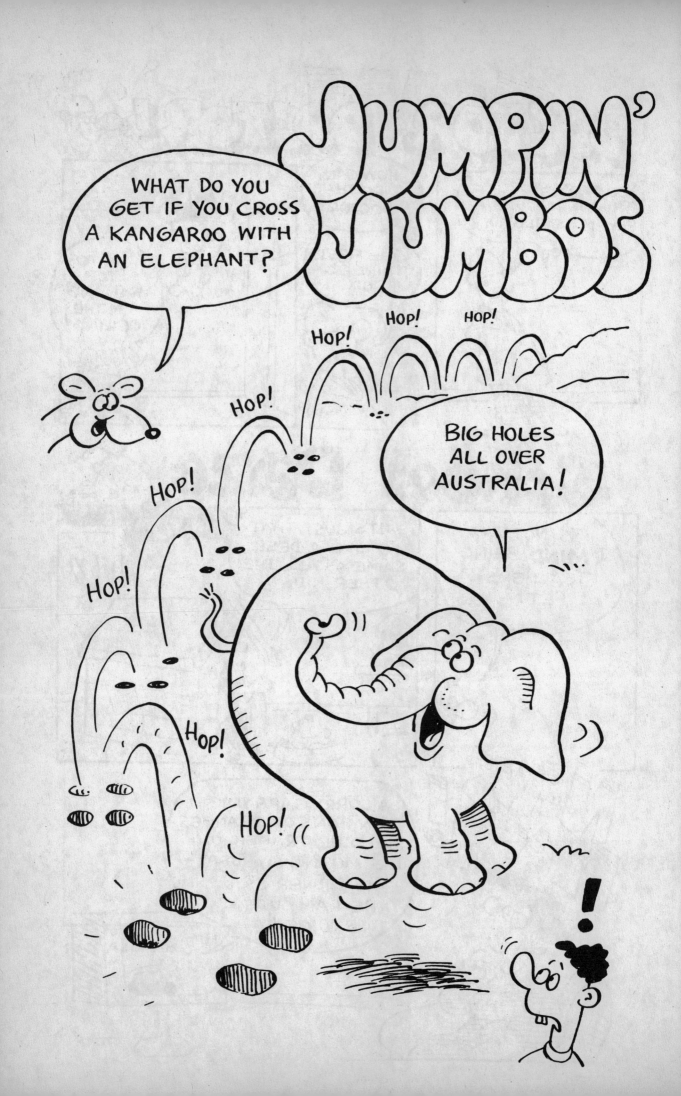

SILLY STRIPS...

Stupid Sid's
RED LETTER DAY..

DANGER!
KIDS AT SCHOOL!!

JESTER MINUTE!

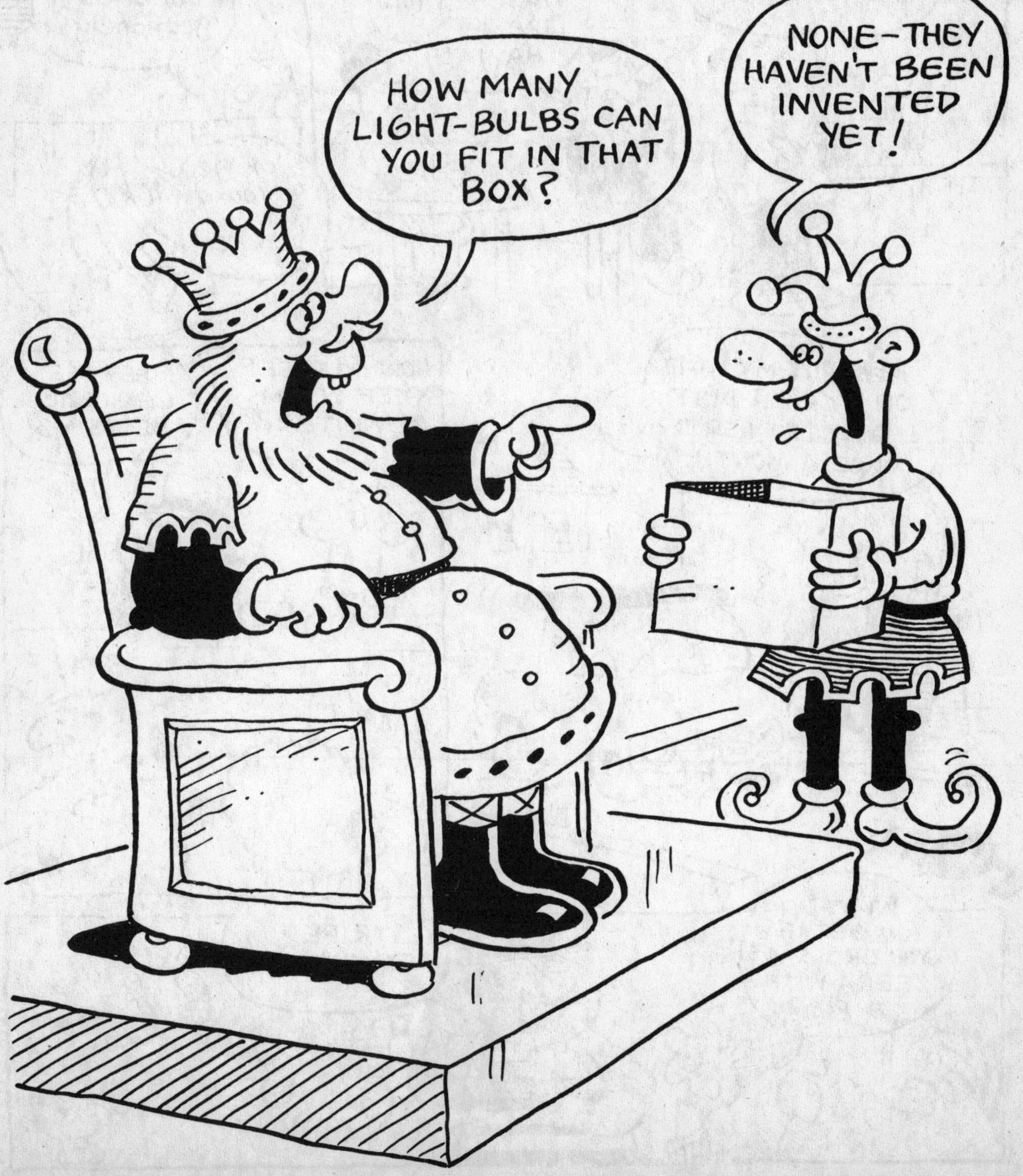

a Tall story

Stupid Sid's
DO-IT-YOURSELF PAGE...

O.K, So you can't take any more —
And who can blame you?.... so, this page
is designed either to let you have a rest,
OR,
if you think you can do any better,
now's your chance...

SiLLY STRIPS....

Light Relief...

Join the Dots with **Stupid Sid...**

•100

•7

•98   •99   •11   •36   •19
    •97   •3
•6   •20   •5
•21   •96   •25   •45   •44
    •15   •95   •1   •2   •12
        •8   •3
•94   •48   •4   •46
•49 10 •93   •92 •47   •9   •34   •43
        •14
•31   •24   •18   •42   •7
        •23   •28
            •91
            •27
•50   •22   •30   •35   •41
•32   •29   •36
    •64   •53   •90
•65   •33   •89   •57
•51   •16   •38   •55 •37
        •52   •56   •88
•66   •63   •54   •60   •40
•76   •39   •59   •58
•77 •67   •62 •69 •71   •83   •73
    •79 •74 •61   •81   •85   •87
•78   •75   •70   •72   •84
    •68   •80   •82   •86

Did you hear about...

...the cat who took First Prize at the Bird Show?..... he ate the Prize Canary!

PURR-FECT!

....the man who invented a gadget for seeing through solid walls?... he called it a 'window'!!

looks good to me!

...the farmer who gave hot water to his chickens?..... they laid hard-boiled eggs!!

yum!

....the school swot who killed more flies than anybody else in his class?

OW!

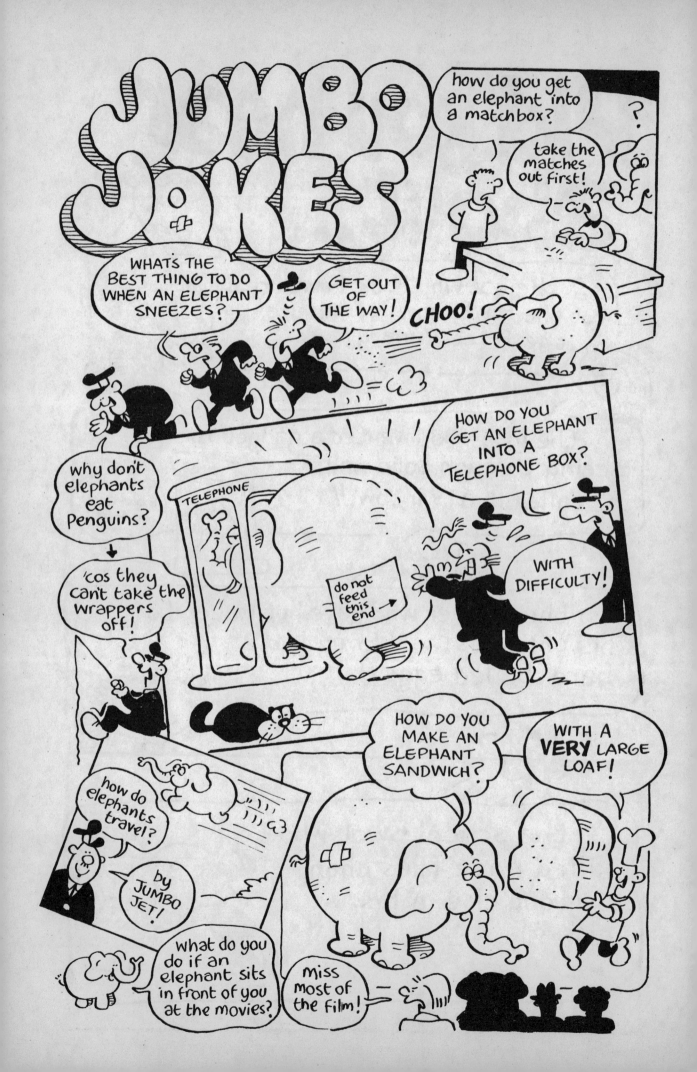

Stupid Sid — the DOZY KID!

Roland Butter...

... the WACKY WAITER!

WELL, FOLKS, THAT'S IT,
I'M AFRAID.... THE END OF
THE LINE.... YES, IT'S....SOB...
GOODBYE TIME.... SOB....

I HOPE YOU'VE ENJOYED THE
FEAST OF FUN.... SOB....
AS MUCH AS I HAVE....

THERE'S NOT A LOT TO SAY,
REALLY.... SOB....

.... EXCEPT....

.... WHY NOT TURN TO
THE FRONT OF THE
BOOK AND
START AGAIN?!

start **again**? he's got to be **kidding!**